GOLDEN VERSE

Golden Verse is a collection of feel-good poetry, inspired by the author's passionate love of life and nature.

Born in July 1949 (birth sign Leo), Denise Hackett was brought-up in the village of Cantley where she attended the local secondary school. As a child she won first prize in a best handwriting contest and was also awarded certificates for History.

A housewife, she has two sons, a daughter and five grandchildren. She met her second husband Clifford through work and they live in the village of Spotbrough. They married on St Valentine's Day, 2002, and the happy event is described in the poem 'Valentine Wedding' which features in this book. Photos from their 'fairytale' wedding appeared in many magazines as well as the local newspaper. The best man, maids of honour and the bridesmaids all work at Panache, Denise's favourite hair salon which she visits every week.

Apart from poetry, Denise has recently begun writing short stories. She also adores travel, music and dancing, and takes a keen interest in local history.

Husband Clifford persuaded Denise to have *Golden Verse* published, and although this is her first book her work has already appeared in anthologies and on the internet. A selection of her poems are on display in the Poets' Hall of Fame museum in Sittingbourne, Kent (under the name of Denise Frost).

GOLDEN VERSE

Denise Hackett

ARTHUR H. STOCKWELL LTD.
Torrs Park   Ilfracombe   Devon
Established 1898
www.ahstockwell.co.uk

© Denise Hackett, 2003
First published in Great Britain, 2003
All rights reserved.
No part of this publication may be reproduced
or transmitted in any form or by any means,
electronic or mechanical, including photocopy,
recording, or any information storage and
retrieval system, without permission
in writing from the copyright holder.

British Library Cataloguing-in-Publication Data.
A catalogue record for this book is available
from the British Library.

ISBN 0 7223 3535-0
Printed in Great Britain by
Arthur H. Stockwell Ltd.
Torrs Park   Ilfracombe
Devon

Contents

Spring Appears	7
Romance	8
The Spirit of Christmas	9
Christmas Noel	10
The Moonlight	11
The Video	12
In the Attic	13
Christmas Joy	14
Have Faith	15
The Curiosity Shop	16
The Red Dress	17
Home is Where the Heart is	18
Cornwall's Beauty	19
Inspirations	20
Elegant Lady	21
Young Love	22
Motherhood	23
Intimate	24
Fulfillment	25
Broken Love Affair	26
Sad and Lonely	27
Love's Enchanting Land	28
Path of Gold	29
Valentine Wedding	30
Pennies From Heaven	31
Christmas Cheer	32

Spring Appears

Springtime's just around the corner now,
Winter's landscapes made a silent bow;
The cuckoo calls its mating sound,
Casting peace and tranquillity around.

The crocus flourishes, its petals unfurl,
Those snowdrops like the dewy pearls;
Fluffy lambs are born, they skip along,
Oh! such relief from Winters long.

Translucent waters, Spring light fresh streams,
So refreshing it sparkles and gleams;
The longer evenings that had come forth,
Cold winds disappear from the north.

Filigree of the forming trees,
Brightness of sunshine, calming breeze;
Woodland splendour, gardens adoring,
All the glory on a Spring light morning.

Romance

Romance is a sophisticated form,
Of feeling somewhat now reborn;
You look into each other's eyes,
And lovebirds almost fill the skies.

Romantic dreams you have at night,
Until the next time you capture sight,
Of your loved one fond and true,
Bringing shadows into brighter view.

Romance turns thoughts to reality,
And fantasy to normality;
Caring, sharing, holding one another close,
Feelings then are just the most.

Treasured memories when you first met,
Are special times you never forget;
Romance is something which sweeps you off your feet,
Making life now seem complete.

The Spirit of Christmas

The atmosphere so glowing and warm,
On this eve before Christmas morn;
Blissful harmony fills the air,
Christmas joy a time to share.

Children's hearts so gleeful,
Spirits high in the night lull;
Cards and decorations adorn the wall,
As through the windowpane the snow does fall.

Such sheer magic does surround,
As crispy snowflakes coat the ground;
The Christmas tree fills the limelight,
As the carol singers disappear into the night.

The fire's glow makes shadows round the room,
Children's Santa's coming now soon;
Oh! the mystery of the Christmas story,
But the wonderful legend stands in full glory.

Christmas Noel

Noel the yuletide name of old,
Christmas tradition, stories unfold;
The glowing candles light the room,
Like June roses in full bloom.

The gifts are stacked under the tree,
Such joyful faces full of glee;
Holly twigs spread on the shelf,
Bringing Christmas a warming wealth.

Those fairy lights sparkle and shine,
Treasured memories so divine,
Of the year's adventures past,
But the time has flown so fast.

Christmas spirits, hearts fulfilled,
In this season of goodwill;
Precious golden times luxuriously spent,
On this eve, the Advent.

The Moonlight

The moonlight shining into the bedroom gleaming,
Shining over as I lay there dreaming;
The milky sheen of the silken moon,
Beaming bright before daybreak soon.

You look down from the darkened sky,
Your shimmering beauty so blyth;
The stars surround you in the sapphire skies,
Looking over a newborn's cries.

Your shimmer then hide behind your clouds,
With your thousand stars in crowds;
You tranquil moon whom I adore to see,
Oh! wonderful moonlight what is she?

The Video

The video of our wedding day,
Was so bright and full of gay;
Going to the church in cars supreme,
The bride in glorious array, she looked a dream.

The scene was set, the picture show,
Then in the church the guests did go;
She stole the limelight, her precious day,
Looking radiant they both vowed and prayed.

The man behind the camera caught every moment,
Standing next for marriage enrolment;
Our vicar stood in costume splendid,
In the crowd he gracefully blended.

The happy couple now bride and groom,
Glowing thoughts inside them loom;
This wondrous day spent together,
In the glorious Springtime weather.

In the Attic

Stored away all Childhood things,
Fairy for the Christmas tree has lost her wings;
The old rocking horse now still in the corner,
Old photo albums, glowing thoughts brought warmer.

Those tatty books with pages missing,
Dressing-up clothes to look sheer bliss in;
Painted dolls lay sad and unkept,
In their cot for years haven't slept.

Teddy bear has lost his ear,
Shadows on the wall appear;
All the toys kept up here now,
As through each box I deeply plough.

A farmyard set still intact,
Neatly stored, dolls in boxes trimmly packed;
Oh! the memories of these playthings I see,
Bring back the laughter and all the glee.

Christmas Joy

The radiant fireside glow warms the room,
Joyous merriment already looms;
The Christmas tree stands with a decorative enchantment,
The holly leaves and sparkling wines bring the enhancement;
Those stockings over the fireside dangle,
Childhood dreams in your heart do untangle.

Magic moments preciously spent,
Whispers of an aromatic scent,
Fills the air on Christmas Eve,
As welcome visitors drink their mead,
The fairy lights set upon the tree,
Shining brightly for all to see.

Those garlands to and fro do sway,
As the clouds of darkness meet the day;
Children sleep waiting for Santa's call,
As the clock chimes away upon the wall.

Christmas season, the golden hours,
Fairy lights and poinsettia flowers;
The scene is set into the night,
As the snowflakes fall all crispy white.

Have Faith

When life treats you very rough,
Hang on in there and greet it tough;
When you've been dealt with such a raw deal,
You wonder how all others feel.

Looking on to all your ails,
Find true strength if all else fails;
Live each day to full potential,
Pray to God for help it is essential;
Fight the good fight and get stronger each time,
Life can be fun matured like wine.

Don't despair, all will be well in the end,
Our true wishes we send you as a friend;
You'll gain strength from within each day,
We'll pray for you for sunshine your way.

The Curiosity Shop

There it stood the old Curiosity Shop, prim,
In that little square so neat and so trim;
I walked inside, such fascination I saw,
Oh! I could hardly wait to round the shop explore.

There were ornate tapestries, jugs and earthenware,
Olde-worlde dolls standing there;
Fancy mirrors, pictures hung rare,
Old heirlooms, a Chippendale chair.

I browsed along to see what I could find,
Interesting ornaments, all different kinds,
A quaint little showcase, and now seek you shall find.

A piece of jewellery Whitby jet,
Something I've wanted always to get;
Tattered old postcards stood in a tin,
I rummaged through to see what was in.

The Red Dress

I fell in love with that enchanting dress,
Pure chiffon, frilly, only the very best;
It stood in the window, such a dream,
That exquisite dress adds lustre to the scene.

My heart I set upon that dress fair,
Such pure magic, full of flair;
It had a full skirt and was lavishly made,
Vivid red of the brightest shade.

Oh! I must buy my fairytale dress,
Then the people around me I'll surely impress;
Like Cinderella going to the ball,
Over my shoulder I'll wear a shawl.

Rows of frills, and puffed-up sleeves,
Pretty petal-shaped leaves;
Oh! this dress I do adore,
In all its glory, who could want for more!

Home is Where the Heart is

The home is a place of love,
It starts out like a rosebud,
Then opens out and grows supreme,
That wonderful home of hidden dreams.

We travel far and wide,
But back home we like to reside,
To return to our house a welcoming sight,
Especially upon a Winter's night.

The glowing fireside where we sit,
A picture of happiness we do depict;
Fill your home with lots of love — be content,
In your castle, it's heaven-sent.

The only place to relax and be free,
In your home, your luxury;
Thinking of the celebrations,
Here you've had with your relations.

The family house it reigns supreme,
A secluded place, a cosy scene;
Your heart will always stay there,
A wondrous place beyond compare.

Cornwall's Beauty

Cornwall has idyllic views,
A fond place I like to choose;
The sleepy harbours become transformed,
As the sunset overrides the dawn;
In nestled villages do appear.

The mild dewy ocean, with translucent waters,
Those classy hotels with all the porters;
And seashore flats built along the bay,
For visitors to admire on their way.

Winding lanes that are never ending,
Down cliff steps bathers descending;
Wondrous beaches peachy soft to feel,
Hidden beauty this picture does steal.

The charisma of it all,
A place to truly love and adore;
So sedate this Riviera town,
It really does wear the crown.

There is no comparison to match it – this is the most,
To me it really deserves the toast;
English heritage, and a glorious coastline,
A place to honour so divine.

Inspirations

I gather inspirations as I travel round,
A wealth of beauty is to be found;
Countryside mellow and warm,
Seashore coastline serene after dawn.

Inspirational thoughts I do gather from within,
From this glorious world we all live in;
Wherever you may wander treasured gems are found,
All delicately bustling all around.

Lucky heather blowing in the breeze,
Petite bluebells grow in-between the trees;
Buttercups and daisies now showing,
An abundance of flowers to overflowing.

Squirrels nestle in woodland glades,
All nature's creatures softly laze;
Farmyards booming work a plenty,
Mansions stood owned by gentry.

Elegant Lady

Such elegance that Lady fair,
This I really must declare;
Stylish clothes cut so trim,
Superb wear to be seen in.

She glides along so graciously,
And glares at others hazily;
Such elegance within her soul,
As beautiful as roses in a bowl;
She was born with all the flair,
Chooses clothes with special care.

Bold colours, height of fashion,
This dear lady has the passion;
Wearing outfits, a superb range,
Every time she has a change.

Young Love

Two young people fell in love,
Deep in love more than anyone could;
They tried to hide their emotion,
But truly felt deep devotion;
Both were very shy and possessive,
Even to the point of being aggressive.

Their relationship was sometimes stormy and erratic,
But they sealed their love automatic;
They would dance the night away,
Then travel home near light of day.

They had rows when tempers flared,
But underneath they truly cared;
None could match this loving pair,
Full of romance, no despair.

They're very possessive towards each other,
But that is a feeling one must discover;
They've courted strong now for a few years,
Sometimes ending up in tears!

Motherhood

A mother's love for her children is incomparable that's true,
She worships her family from the moment they're due;
That warmth of feeling deep inside,
A mother's thoughts are full of pride.

She stands and welcomes you home from school,
It is always one of her golden rules;
Being there to welcome you in,
Feeling a part of her next of kin;
Her warm smile and loving open arms,
Filling the house with aromatic charm.

Such momentous moments so precious she steals,
True heartfelt emotions she feels;
Reading bedtime stories tucked up in bed,
As you lay down your weary head.

As you slumber off into golden dreams,
Mother slips away from the scene;
But next day she's there to care for you,
Wonderful mother so loving and true.

Intimate

Intimate moments spent with you,
Brings glowing feelings into view;
Relaxing, loving, talking, sweet,
Making love before you go to sleep.

Laying in each other's arms,
Feeling warmth from my lover's charms;
Touching your cheeks, smoothing your brow,
Golden moments spent with you now.

Your velvety soft skin adorns the pillow,
Your arms droop down like a weeping willow;
A lustrous sheen in your hair,
Your loving touch beyond compare.

Precious time spent lovingly together,
Are cherished times to always treasure;
Horizons always come to view,
From this feeling of love I get with you.

Fulfillment

Fulfillment in life is so precious to hold,
Your spirit really needs to be bold;
You're really blessed when you feel fulfilled,
It comes from being very strong willed.

Great expectations are what you feel,
Glimpses of paradise in your thoughts do show,
Fires of contentment with a warming glow;
If you fill your life to overflowing,
Quality high forever showing.

Essence of beauty bestowed within,
That's where fulfilment really begins;
Always tread the path steadfastly,
Changes views on life so vastly.

Bringing joy to everyone you meet,
Making all your lives complete;
You feel fulfilled when you've done these things,
Like the dove with golden wings.

Broken Love Affair

To feel so rejected makes one feel so blue,
Wondering to yourself why you're so empty inside,
And need someone to reassure you and confide;
No one understands how it feels to be jilted,
Like a flower when it's wilted.

People try to console you but to no avail,
You walk round looking sad and pale;
All the glory now has gone,
No overtures for your love song.

You think will my wedding ever happen real,
Such precious memories of our love to steal;
Being let down before the great day,
Leaves me nothing else to say.

Sad and Lonely

Don't feel downhearted,
As your love has now departed;
Have faith and things will change,
Giving you a choice of range;
Feeling lonely and full of despair,
Wondering if people really care.

Sadness is a dreadful state,
Making you think of your cruel fate;
You've stayed on your own so long now,
Making you bitter, causing your head to bow,

Never give up hope your destiny's planned,
You're just waiting for the right man;
When he comes along he'll win your heart,
And never then will you neither part.

Believe in friends, they truly care,
As at your heartstrings people tear;
Don't dismay, just carry on,
Until you meet your love lifelong.

Love's Enchanting Land

Ireland, Oh! Ireland you most romantic land.
The mountains do echo, the streams, lakes all so grand;
The lush green meadows, animals, grazing little lambs at play,
Travelling this glorious land really makes your day.

Those horse and drays meandering down the country lanes,
Lush fields abound, golden fruitful plains;
Rich in its harvest natural from the earth do bring,
An abundance of produce, it makes young want to sing.

With love in your heart rejoice,
Call out to the majestic Isle singing in grand voice;
Cupid's arrow cast his magic spell here,
With Irish leprechauns you see quaint fairies appear.

Dancing in the gardens, the children all so happy,
Driving home for Irish lunch, better make it snappy;
I have that affinity with Ireland, the Emerald Isles,
Oh! such a blessing to adorn a thousand smiles.

Path of Gold

Some have wealth beyond compare,
Others are driven to despair,
Trying to build up their dreams,
But life doesn't turn out all it seems.

The path of gold they try to tread,
But are left holding but a thread;
Hopes are just a fantasy,
Never turned to reality.

Hoping, praying to climb the ladder of success,
But with these things they were never blessed;
Faded dreams that turned so plain,
Trying so hard but only in vain.

Not everyone can follow that path of gold,
But try with all your might your spirit bold;
To paint your cloud lined with golden dust,
To pretend so hard, but in God you trust.

Valentine Wedding

Oh! that wonderful golden day,
Our stunning guests all out in beautiful array;
The bride broke with tradition, wore a gown in red and gold,
Moving away from the repetitive mould.

The bridesmaids stood so serene in their gold satin dresses,
With filigree ringlets, such perfect golden stresses;
The bride and groom took vows to our Redeemer on high,
That feeling of grandeur a place nice to be, don't cry!

The tranquil lake and avenue of trees stole the scene,
For the glorious photos, the best to be seen;
The white Rolls-Royce stood so serene,
This fairytale wedding, such a Valentine dream.

Pennies From Heaven

Pennies from heaven just drop from the sky,
Oh! such joyous fantasy makes me want to cry;
Providence will provide whatever the weather,
Even when you aren't so clever.

Pitter, patter, raindrops trickling down the windowpane,
Like pennies from heaven, falling heavy rain.
Freshening the meadows, mountains, lakes supreme.
Glorious paradise, the earth's an artist's dream;
Rainbows appearing in the aftermath of the skies,
When all is now calming as birds flutter by.

Bring me pennies from heaven, to make fruitful my harvest here,
Abundance of love, hope, good health and cheer;
Reign over the land with your streets paved with gold,
Bringing forth avid treasures for everyone to hold.

Christmas Cheer

The Christmas carousel is riding round again,
A year of new beginnings, nothing stays the same;
Christmas in the moonlight fair,
Numerous stars in the sky knowing Winter's there;
Children playing in the snow,
With cheery faces, such a cheeky glow.

Christmas shoppers everywhere, all the stores are full,
Bringing loads of merriment in the Winter chill;
Fairylights adorn the tree,
Bringing joy to you and me.

Christmas is a-coming, singing out Noel,
Oh! this Winter wonderland casts its magic spell;
Snow in the air on snowcapped mountains fell,
The streets are alive, many stories to tell.

Winter wonderland, Christmas joy, in abundance everywhere,
Children so bewildered, their faces in shop windows stare;
An everglade of joyous things,
This is what true Christmas brings.